SCOTNOTES
Number 7

Muriel Spark's
The Prime of Miss Jean Brodie

David S. Robb

D1099286

Association for Scottish Literary Studies 1992

Published by
Association for Scottish Literary Studies
c/o Department of Scottish History
9 University Gardens
University of Glasgow
Glasgow G12 8QH

www.asls.org.uk

First published 1992
Reprinted 1999, 2001, 2002

A CIP catalogue for this title is available from the British Library

ISBN 0 948877 14 6

The Association for Scottish Literary Studies
is in receipt of subsidy from the Scottish Arts Council

THE SCOTTISH ARTS COUNCIL

Typeset by Roger Booth Associates, Hassocks, West Sussex
Printed by Ritchie (UK) Ltd, Kilmarnock

CONTENTS

Editors' Foreword   v
Note on References   vi

MURIEL SPARK AND HER NOVELS
    Spark and Scotland   1
    The Kind of Novels She Writes   2
    A Brief Glimpse of her Life-Story   3
    A Brief Glimpse of her Other Novels   4

THE EVENTS IN THE NOVEL
    How the Story is Not Told   7
    How the Book Unfolds These Events   9
    The Story-Telling Compromise   11
    When Is 'Now'?   11

THE NOVEL AND THE PERIOD IN WHICH IT IS SET
    The 1930s   16
    Between Two Wars   17
    Life in the 1930s   18
    Jean Brodie and Fascism   19
    Jean Brodie and Hitler   22

RELIGION IN THE NOVEL
    Sandy's Conversion   25
    Jean Brodie as Justified Sinner   28
    Sandy and Catholicism   31

ASSESSING JEAN BRODIE
    What Are We to Make of Her?   34
    What Do Other Characters make of Her?   36
    Brodies, Old and New   38
    Perhaps the Author Might Help Us?   40

SANDY STRANGER AND THE BRODIE SET
    Two Heroines? — Jean Brodie and Sandy   43
    The World of the Brodie Set   46
    The Strangeness of Sandy Stranger   48

DAYDREAMS, STORIES AND TRUTH

Imagining the World Around Us 50
Spinning Yarns and Telling Tales 52
Is It Safe to Trust the Imagination? 54

SELECT BIBLIOGRAPHY 57

EDITORS' FOREWORD

The *Scotnotes* booklets are a series of study guides to major Scottish writers and literary texts that are likely to be elements within literature courses. They are aimed at senior pupils in secondary schools and students in further education colleges and colleges of education. Each booklet in the series is written by a person who is not only an authority on the particular writer or text but also experienced in teaching at the relevant levels in schools or colleges. Furthermore, the editorial board, composed of members of the Schools and Further Education Committee of the Association for Scottish Literary Studies, considers the suitability of each booklet for the students in question.

For many years there has been a shortage of readily accessible critical notes for the general student of Scottish literature. *Scotnotes* has grown as a series to meet this need, and provides students with valuable aids to the understanding and appreciation of the key writers and major texts within the Scottish literary tradition.

Lorna Borrowman Smith
Ronald Renton

NOTE ON REFERENCES

The page references in this study guide are to the Penguin Books edition of the novel, first published in 1965.

MURIEL SPARK AND HER NOVELS

Spark and Scotland

Muriel Spark has acquired perhaps the greatest international reputation of any Scots-born writer of her generation. In large part this is due, of course, to the sheer excellence and originality of her writing, but has probably been helped, at least to some extent, by the fact that she has lived her adult life outside Scotland. During the Sixties, when her literary reputation became fully established, she seemed part of the rather glamorous world of art, literature, film, *et cetera* which flourished in the cities where she made her homes: London, New York, Rome.

She would appear to have turned her back on her native Scotland – apart, that is, from recreating it in memory in *The Prime of Miss Jean Brodie*. Hardly any of her other novels make use of Scottish settings, nor do Scottish characters figure with any great prominence in them. She makes the hero of *The Ballad of Peckham Rye*, published in 1960 (a year before *The Prime of Miss Jean Brodie*), a Scotsman but the novel is set, as the title suggests, in Peckham in south London. A recent novel, *Symposium*, is partly set in St Andrews. And that is about it. There would seem to be room for doubt whether or not we should regard her as being, in any real sense, a Scottish writer. Even *Jean Brodie* was first published not in this country but in the American magazine, *The New Yorker*.

Yet the situation is not quite so simple as that, for Muriel Spark has clearly retained a strong sense of her Scottish origins. *The Prime of Miss Jean Brodie* is extremely detailed and convincing not just about the geography and features of Edinburgh and its surrounding area but also (more importantly) about the subtle turns of speech and of mental outlook which are characteristic of the city: her continued sense of involvement with the place could be demonstrated from that book alone. Also, it is possible for those who have read widely in Scottish literature to find echoes of various earlier writers in her work; it seems likely that Robert Louis Stevenson, James Hogg and the Border Ballads have all made their mark on this expatriate novelist.

Her sense of still being Scottish is confirmed, moreover, by articles and interviews published at various times in her career. In a brief account entitled 'What Images Return', she noted down her thoughts on returning to Edinburgh for a few weeks to be real-life teacher would never have contemplated. The novel is full of invention, whatever its basis in life.)

While a pupil at Gillespie's, Muriel Spark was already writing poems, and became noted ('famous'?) throughout the school for her literary ardour. In 1937, however, ardour of another kind led her, at the age of nineteen, to run off and marry an older man, going with him to Rhodesia. They had a son, but the marriage failed and after a divorce she returned to wartime London and got a job with the Foreign Office writing propaganda. After the war she was a prominent official in the Poetry Society for a time.

From 1951, religion began to play an increasingly important part in her outlook and values and she became a Catholic in 1954. A year later she was invited by the publishing firm Macmillan to write a novel and so her first novel, *The Comforters*, was published in 1957. It has been followed by a steady stream of others: her nineteenth, *Symposium*, was published in the autumn of 1990. Her reputation rests on these novels, but she is also the author of much else, including poetry, biography, literary criticism, short stories, a play and also a book for children. While there appears to have been a certain measure of coincidence in the fact that her first novel was written not long after the period of personal religious upheaval which finally brought her to the Catholic faith, there can also be little doubt that her finding of herself as a Catholic was really necessary to allow the great and sudden outpouring of books which followed *The Comforters*. She herself has said that 'I find I speak far more with my own voice as a Catholic' and that 'I wasn't able to work and do any of my writing until I became a Catholic'. This does not mean, however, that her novels have got to be understood only from an orthodox Catholic point of view.

A Brief Glimpse of her Other Novels

No single feature marks out a Muriel Spark novel from novels by anyone else but her books are nevertheless distinctively her own. They are often about a clear-cut group of characters, a group, furthermore, which is defined partly by some shared quality but also partly by something more outward, often even a geographical location. Her novels frequently convey a strong sense of the place in which they are set, and (almost as strongly) of the period in which they are located. Thus *The Prime of Miss Jean Brodie* is about a group of young girls beginning to learn about life, but it is also about a whole school community and about Edinburgh, too. *The Girls of Slender Means* is about a group of young unmarried women beginning to make a life for themselves at the end of the war: they live in a girls' hostel and the novel is steeped in a sense of London at that particular moment in its history. *The Bachelors* is about a group of bachelors, in London once again during the late 50s; but it is also about a rather strange group of spiritualists. *A Far Cry From Kensington* is also about London life, in the early 50s this time, and it is set particularly in the world of publishers' offices and of bed-sit life. And so on. Each novel takes a rather narrowly circumscribed group of people and works itself out within limits that feel just slightly artificial, even though we usually feel that Spark is depicting her chosen, constricted slice of life with great realism. The most extreme instances of this tendency towards narrow 'worlds' in her fiction are her second novel, *Robinson*, which is set on a desert island and has only five main characters, and *The Driver's Seat*, which has only one main figure and tells the tale of that character's last thirty-six hours of life – what she does, the people she meets, *et cetera*.

As an almost natural consequence of this tendency towards strictly-defined subject-matter, Muriel Spark's novels are usually brief and concise. *The Prime of Miss Jean Brodie* is a fairly representative length. Only one of these novels is really much longer than that: *The Mandelbaum Gate* seems less tightly hemmed in and is more like a normal modern popular novel in size. On the other hand, quite a few of her novels are notably shorter than *Jean Brodie* and read almost like rather long short stories. This, too, has a tendency to make us try to think about them more: we feel that we might be able to hold them complete in our minds and see the patterns which they contain.

That they are meant to be thought about is something we come to realise as we read them, because they usually seem designed to do something over and above just telling stories about people like us and about events in our world. Even the most 'realistic' of them has a quality of the not-strictly-realistic. It isn't just that we are always very aware of there being an author who is organising her material in a rather unpredictable way and who is selecting words in a very stylish manner, but also the events in the story (the 'matter' as opposed to the 'manner') usually have at least a slight tinge of the unlikely about them. Compared with other Spark novels, *The Prime of Miss Jean Brodie* has very little of this stretching of the bounds of probability but even here it is to be encountered, I think, in the way Miss Brodie develops and in the climax of the story itself. How likely is it that a middle-aged schoolmistress will try to encourage her pupils to sleep with another member of staff, or be 'betrayed' by a pupil in circumstances similar to what we find here? None of it is impossible; it is just all rather unlikely, when one stops to think about it. This becomes clearer when one thinks instead of Miss Kay and of the real-life relationship between her and the young Muriel Spark. Christina Kay was obviously rather an unusual teacher (an unusually *good* teacher) but she was not Miss Brodie; the differences between her life and personality and those of Jean Brodie rest in what we might call the melodramatic features of the fictional character – the unconventional extremes of her mind and actions.

The unlikelinesses of this novel are slight, however, compared with what we find elsewhere in Spark's fiction. In *The Comforters*, one of the characters is a novelist who is writing a novel on her typewriter: she sometimes hears the sound of a mysterious typewriter and a voice speaking the words of *this* novel, and becomes aware that she is *in* a novel which is being written. To take another example, *Memento Mori* is based on the idea of a group of elderly people who receive anonymous phone calls in which a voice tells them to remember they must die: the nearest to an explanation that the novel provides is that the caller is Death himself. At the end of *The Hothouse by the East River* we find that the characters whom we had thought were merely rather neurotic inhabitants of 1960s New York are all ghosts of people who had been killed in London during the war by a German rocket. *The Driver's Seat* tells the story of Lise, another neurotic, who goes on holiday to pick up a man not for the amorous reason we are expecting but to force him to murder her. And so on. These are perhaps the most extreme instances but all Muriel Spark's fiction can be found to combine a detailed accuracy in depicting everyday life, and a purely fictional, invented fantasy-world. What changes from book to book is the proportion of each which is offered. In the end, we are likely to feel that even what seems to be the real world is just another form of fantasy.

THE EVENTS IN THE NOVEL

How the Story is Not Told

The following is an account of the most prominent events, mentioned or implied in the novel; it is not an account of the sequence of events as the novel offers them. It begins with the earliest event relevant to the main characters, and ends with the most up-to-date.

Jean Brodie is born in 1890. At the beginning of the First World War (1914–18) she becomes engaged but her fiancé Hugh is killed: she says that he dies a week before the armistice (which was signed on 11 November 1918) and that he was only twenty-two – in which case he was six years younger than she. The girls who will become 'the Brodie set' are born in 1920 and when they are ten years of age, in 1930, they enter Jean Brodie's class in the Junior School of Marcia Blaine School in Edinburgh. This is the first of the two years for which they will have her as class teacher, during which time she largely ignores the curriculum prescribed by the school and passes on, instead, a haphazard but intoxicating mixture of facts and opinions peculiar to herself. She thereby dominates the lives of her new pupils. She picks out a group of favourites whom she invites to her home for tea and makes her confidantes, telling them of her private life and her battles within the school. She gives them a sense of group identity, but dominates them. She declares that she has just entered what she calls her 'prime' (she is forty years old) and believes that she is therefore at her maximum effectiveness as a teacher and at her very best as a woman. It is during this first year with her – in March 1931 – that she takes the class on the walk through the Old Town of Edinburgh (27–40).

The second of the two years with her (autumn 1931 till early summer 1932) is marked by the girls' preoccupation with sex: they begin to suspect a liaison between Miss Brodie and Teddy Lloyd, the art master. In the late autumn of 1931, however, Miss Brodie begins an affair with Gordon Lowther, the music master, whom she does not prefer to Teddy Lloyd but who, unlike Lloyd, is unmarried. In late Easter, 1932, Sandy Stranger encounters a flasher by the Water of Leith, and falls in love with the police-woman who interviews her about it.

The girls move out of Jean Brodie's class and into the Senior School in autumn 1932, when they are about twelve years old, and respond well to the new subjects and teachers. Miss Brodie keeps up the connection by trying to learn Greek with them, but abandons it in the late spring of 1933 (84). She is also keeping up her relationship with Lowther, and the girls visit the two of them, on Saturdays, at his house in Cramond. During this year, too, the girls begin to be invited to Lloyd's studio in his home. He begins to paint Rose Stanley in the early summer of 1933. Soon after this a nightdress is discovered under Lowther's pillow, and the fact reported to the headmistress who has been looking for an excuse to get rid of Miss Brodie: this accusation fails in removing Miss Brodie, but results in the removal of Lowther from the position of church choirmaster (94–95).

By autumn 1935, Miss Brodie has begun to confide specially in Sandy Stranger, as during the game of golf (105–108). Also, Sandy, at the age of fifteen, has begun to be interested in religion and aware of the Calvinist traditions of Edinburgh. As they enter the fourth form at around the age of sixteen, the girls are beginning to encounter boys, after school, as described at the opening of the book. Also in their fourth year, Joyce Emily Hammond joins the school. Lowther unexpectedly marries Miss Lockhart, the science teacher, and the 'Brodie set' increase their involvement with Teddy Lloyd and his family. The girls' last year at school is session 1937–38, during which Joyce Emily Hammond is befriended separately by Miss Brodie who persuades her to go off to fight in the Spanish Civil War, on the Fascist side. Joyce goes but is killed on the way. Soon after leaving school, in the summer of 1938, Sandy has a brief affair with Lloyd and begins to become interested in Catholicism. She also discovers that Joyce had been persuaded to go to Spain by Miss Brodie. Sandy 'betrays' Miss Brodie to Miss Mackay, accusing her of teaching Fascism, and Miss Brodie is forced to leave at the end of the session, in the summer of 1939. Sometime between the 'betrayal' and Miss Brodie's quitting teaching, Sandy joins the Catholic Church (125).

Rose marries soon after leaving school. Another of the girls in the group, Mary MacGregor, dies in a hotel fire in 1943, at around the time that another of the set, Jenny Gray, gets married (81). Sandy has her conversation with Miss Brodie in the Braid Hills Hotel in autumn 1945. Miss Brodie is already ill, 'suffering from an internal growth' (56), but lives long enough to hear the news of Sandy's entering a convent. The religious order she joins enforces very strict seclusion. She writes a successful book of psychology and morality called *The Transfiguration of the Commonplace* which makes her famous and which causes her to be visited by interested people from all over the world, for which she is given a special dispensation. Meanwhile, the other girls have all followed their different lives and we occasionally glimpse them: Eunice Gardner, in 1959, plans with her husband to return to Edinburgh for the Festival (26–27); Monica Douglas visits Sandy (now 'Sister Helena of the Transfiguration') 'in the late nineteen-fifties' and recalls seeing Teddy Lloyd and Miss Brodie kissing in the art room (55); Monica also visits Miss Brodie a few weeks before her death within a year of the war ending (63); Jenny Gray experiences a sudden unexpected flood of sexual interest and desire one day in Rome when she is 'nearly forty' in, say, 1959 (80–81) – she has become 'an actress of moderate reputation'; in the last few pages of the book, visits to Sandy are made by Rose Stanley, Monica Douglas (whose marriage is breaking up), Jenny Gray, and Eunice Gardner during the year after her visit to the Edinburgh Festival. The period up to and around 1960 is the latest phase from which we catch glimpses of the lives of these characters, but, occasionally, we are reminded of yet later phases still, such as the 'later days' when Jenny looks back to her sudden passion for her Rome acquaintance. When the book first appeared in 1961, however, most of the latest episodes were located in the immediate past (practically the present) of its first readers.

How the Book Unfolds These Events

The chain of events outlined in the previous section is the 'historical' sequence, involving this group of characters, which we are able to imagine as a result of reading the book. As we read, we probably cannot get the picture quite so clear as this account, which has been worked out with some care involving deliberate searching through the book, and deducing dates and sequences from clues and implications, as well as from direct statements. Such a process is not the same as 'reading' the book. Nevertheless, as we read and try to comprehend all that the book has to offer, our minds automatically work to piece together the 'history' of the characters. We do this with any novel that we read, but the impulse to do so in this case is particularly strong because the novel is noticeably full of very precise (and often rather unexpected) snippets of information about dates and about the distance in time between one event and another:

'I dare say I'll not get a seat. This is nineteen-thirty-six. The age of chivalry is past.' (10)

Mary MacGregor, lumpy, with merely two eyes, a nose and a mouth like a snowman, who was later famous for being stupid and always to blame and who, at the age of twenty-three, lost her life in a hotel fire, ... (13–14)

It is seven years, thought Sandy, since I betrayed this tiresome woman. (60)

'I feel I'm past it,' said Jenny. This was strangely true, and she did not again experience her early sense of erotic wonder in life until suddenly one day when she was nearly forty ... There was nothing whatever to be done about it, for Jenny had been contentedly married for sixteen years past ... (80–81)

[Sandy] thought of Miss Brodie eight years ago sitting under the elm tree telling her first simple love story ... (119)

Such information does several things for us. It adds greatly to our sense of the sheer reality of the story we are being told: it is so very precise, and the time-patterns it implies seem so compli-cated, that we tend to believe that only real life could produce these details. At another level of our response, though, we know perfectly well that these details, like everything else in the book, have been thought up by an author, and they add to our belief, which is created by much else in the book besides, that it is a particularly carefully thought-out work, full of controlled com-plexities which we can discover with patient reading and thought. This belief adds to our trust in the author, helping us to respond to her work with a care and respect to match her own. (Clearly, Muriel Spark worked out a very detailed chronology, rather like the one given above, before ever putting pen to paper.) Perhaps most powerfully of all, the network of time-references gives the powerful impression that these characters really did have lives of their own from which apparently disconnected little details can be picked out and offered to us. Thus, the same device operates simultaneously to strengthen our awareness of an author, and to increase our sense of characters as 'real' and independent of any author.

In addition, the feeling that these characters lived real lives in

historical (as opposed to fictional) time just like us enables us –
and, indeed, encourages us – to relate the incidents of their lives
to the real history of the Europe of the 1930s, to which so many
other references in the novel direct us in any case. This 'solidity of
chronology' teams up with various other 'solidities' of which we
are aware as we read – solidity of place (the real Edinburgh is
there, in many details), solidity of speech, solidity of outlook
(these characters think and respond in the way people we know
think and respond) – to make 'realism' a very prominent feature
of the book.

The Story-Telling Compromise

So if Muriel Spark does not begin her story with the birth of Miss
Brodie, nor simply tell it in chronological sequence, what does she
do instead? She compromises between a straightforward chronological telling, and a complex, broken-up version of the chain of
events. If a novelist abandons chronology altogether, the result is
quite extraordinarily hard for a reader to follow. Muriel Spark
clearly wishes her novel to be, among other things, entertaining,
and she does not want to make things unpleasantly hard for her
readers. So, she concentrates on one portion of her total subject-
matter – the years spent by the girls in Marcia Blaine School
between 1930 and 1938 – and treats that as, by and large, a
chronological narrative, inserting all the other information
relating to times both much earlier and much later than this, as
she goes along. (Nevertheless, we should regard the entire sweep
of time, from the youth of Jean Brodie to the present-day
existences of the surviving characters, as the story which is being
told. What comes before and after the story of the girls' time at
school is not therefore less important than that section of events.)

When Is 'Now'?

Even that main segment of the story, however, is unfolded with
the complications of out-of-sequence details and episodes. The
opening scene of the book, for example, set at the school gates,
takes place in the spring or early summer of 1936 (we are told
that it is 1936, but the girls are in the fourth form, which they
entered in 1935, so the scene takes place in the second half of the
academic year, before the summer). When we start to read, we

naturally assume that this is the 'now' of the novel, and that we
are starting to read a story of schoolgirls beginning to explore
their relationships with boys – a very natural subject for a novel.
Two important things happen in these opening pages, however,
which swiftly point the book away from any such concern. Firstly,
this 'now' is pushed aside, in the third paragraph of the book, by
information about an earlier phase of the girls' life in school, and
what we are told in this paragraph (which seems at first glance to
be merely a bit of background information to explain their present
friendliness and group-identity) is so unexpected, intriguing,
outrageous and funny that we are naturally inclined to hear more
about that rather than more about the commonplace conversation
with the boys.

> These girls were discovered to have heard of the
> Buchmanites and Mussolini, the Italian Renaissance
> painters, the advantages to the skin of cleansing
> cream and witch-hazel over honest soap and water,
> and the word 'menarche'; the interior decoration of
> the London house of the author of *Winnie the Pooh*
> had been described to them, as had the love lives of
> Charlotte Bronte and of Miss Brodie herself. (5)

This unexpected education is not only associated with a Miss
Brodie (whose name is already known to us from the book's title),
but the information has apparently been sparked off (no pun
intended) by the mere mention of her name: 'These girls formed
the Brodie set'. This name not only thrusts into the novel the
unexpected theme of unorthodox education, however; it also starts
the process of complicated time-shifts, for we are suddenly told
about not just one period earlier in the lives of these girls, but two:

> These girls formed the Brodie set. That was what
> they had been called even before the headmistress
> had given them the name, in scorn, when they had
> moved from the Junior to the Senior school at the
> age of twelve. (5)

Although we do not realise it at this point, such casual references
to other times, and the folding (as it were) of one time-phase
within another, turn out to be a basic part of the book's method,
until our very sense of what is the 'now' of the novel becomes
blurred and muddled.

The other decisive moment in the opening scene at the gate
occurs a few pages later. Just as the mere mention of the name of

the mysterious Miss Brodie plunges the narrative into un-suspected, and intriguing, switches of time and topic, so the arrival of the lady herself banishes the boys from the book and supplants them, in the interests both of the girls and of us the readers, with her bossy but fascinating personality. Perhaps this is not going to be, after all, a story of young love, and we do not know, at this stage, what kind of story it is going to be instead. (In part, it turns out to be a story of old love, in the sense that the love-life of Jean Brodie, in her early forties, turns out to be important to it. As far as the love experiences of the girls themselves are concerned, interest in sex is merely a phase they go through, and the first sexual involvement any of them has is Sandy's brief affair, just after she leaves school, with that much older man, Teddy Lloyd.)

Not only is Miss Brodie's personality something we naturally want to know more about, but the strange relationship between her and this group of girls is intriguing and has obviously been going on for some considerable time. Thus, we are naturally inclined to hear more about these characters and their past history, for we have clearly come in in the middle of something. The way is thus prepared for what looks like a flashback to the early days of the relationship: the scene of the history lesson under the elm tree is fully satisfying in the picture it gives of the teacher's strange ways.

We are perhaps a little surprised, however, at the end of the chapter, that we are not returned to the girls in their fourth-year phase. Looking ahead to the next chapter, we see that it carries on from where the first had left off. We have been gently moved back to a new 'now', and embark on a basically chronological account of the girls' schooldays. Indeed, we are inclined, especially when first reading the book, to forget the opening scene, and it comes as a further surprise to find ourselves back in it, several chapters later, at the appropriate stage in the girls' school careers. Indeed, once the scene has returned, more than a hundred pages later, Muriel Spark makes it continue as if nothing had intervened: 'They went to the tram-car stop with her. ...' (112)

If we have been expecting a return to the future at the end of the first chapter, we get one, but not the one we expect. Instead of returning to the scene at the gate, we are given a sudden prophetic glimpse of what a still more distant future holds in store for one of the girls: '[Mary MacGregor] who, at the age of twenty-three, lost her life in a hotel fire, ...' It is the first sign of an even more unusual use of time-shift: not only do most novels not suddenly glance forward as this does here, but it is not at all obvious, at this point, why Spark has suddenly chosen to do so.

Any suspicion that this might be a momentary and unimportant forward glance which we can soon forget is thwarted by the opening of the second chapter, which not only continues with and expands upon Mary MacGregor's life and death, but does so in such a way that we feel we are being bounced between time-phases, a little to our bewilderment. The opening paragraph of the chapter suddenly offers a surprisingly full account of her future life, with three expertly chosen details (Mary joins the Wrens, is wretchedly unsuccessful in love, and dies in the fire while on leave) which, together with her touching realisation that her time in Jean Brodie's class was the happiest time of her life, not only seems to sum up her sad and obscure existence as a whole, but almost amounts to a tiny short story on its own. The vividness of those few lines which contain her love-life ('... one occasion of real misery – when her first and last boy-friend, a corporal whom she had known for two weeks, deserted her by failing to turn up at an appointed place and failing to come near her again ...') foreshadows the even more extraordinary fullness of the account of her final moments trapped in the fire. For as long as it takes us to read this paragraph, our 'now' is the later life of poor Mary, and the early days of the little girls as pupils of Jean Brodie become for us (as for Mary) a distant memory.

The pattern of the novel as a whole is thus established: no single 'now' has absolute priority. Although, for the sake of clarity, the backbone of the novel is the narrative of the girls' dealings with Miss Brodie while they are at school, this phase of their lives is never allowed to dominate our attention to the exclusion of all else. What flows from this method of telling the story?

One result is that, in a sense, *none* of the time-phases between which the action shuffles is ever, for us, the real present, the 'now', of the novel. All are clearly being looked back on from some point in the future, even the most up-to-date sections showing Sandy's various interviews in the convent. The story is being told from a 'now' which, for its first readers in 1961, must really have been 'now', for the latest episodes must have taken place (as it were) around 1959–60. This effect holds good, basically, even now (as I think about the novel and write this) thirty years later.

Another effect is that we have a particularly strong sense of someone telling the story. This is surprising here, because if we just look at isolated sentences from the narrative, the novel seems to be written in that very transparent story-telling manner which seems designed to make us concentrate on the lives of the characters without our really being at all aware of someone actually doing the telling. (The decision about how a novel's story is to be told, and who – as it were – is going to tell it, is one of the most fundamental and influential decisions that a novelist has to take. An author may decide that a story is best told by one of the characters, like Nick Carraway in *The Great Gatsby* – or Philip Marlowe in many of Raymond Chandler's thrillers. More often, the story-teller is that privileged, all-knowing being who tells so many tales, the omniscient narrator, but it may be that we have such a strong feeling of personality in the narrator that he/she is a positive presence in our minds as we read. Many of Dickens's novels are 'told' by such a vivid, commenting being, who is often created, in part at least, by a striking, attention-grabbing prose style. Usually, though, the narrator is conspicuous by his/her absence from the forefront of our attention. When we begin to read *The Prime of Miss Jean Brodie*, it looks as if that is going to be case once again.)

THE NOVEL
AND THE PERIOD IN WHICH IT IS SET

The 1930s

We first receive a hint of the strangeness of Jean Brodie, and of the 'education' which she dispenses to her pupils, when, on the novel's first page, the narrator lists the surprising things of which these primary school children have heard. Most of the items on the list are in the nature of general knowledge (obscure as some of the items are) and imply (if they imply anything at all) a lively, female (few men or boys take an interest in cleansing cream and witch-hazel), twentieth-century mind. At the head of the list, however, are two references very much of the Thirties – 'the Buchmanites and Mussolini' – though the latter is admittedly now very much a part of everyone's general knowledge of our century. Nevertheless, the mere fact that Mussolini is regarded as someone of whom twelve-year-olds probably won't have heard implies that he had yet to make his full impact on the world: one suspects that most twelve-year-olds would have heard of him a few years later when, in 1935, he invaded Ethiopia and caused an international crisis and when, a little later still, he formed the Rome-Berlin Axis with Hitler and became increasingly involved in the Spanish Civil War. The Buchmanites, in contrast, were a group now largely lost sight of. They were also called the Oxford Group (there is a reference to this, in passing, on page 43) and were led by an American, Dr Frank Buchman, who advocated the solution to the world's ills through a moral improvement in both private and public life. This religious movement, from 1938 onwards, was called Moral Rearmament. For much of the Thirties, however, it was not widely prominent but was confined, largely, to the private circles of the upper classes. Thus, for twelve-year-old Edinburgh schoolgirls to have heard about them in 1932 was something very surprising indeed.

These two references alone are sufficient to locate the time of the novel in the early 1930s and they are followed by plenty of details which confirm this placing. The girls, newly arrived in Miss Brodie's class, are shown, in another teacher's room, an election poster bearing Stanley Baldwin's photograph: 'Underneath were the words "Safety First"' (10). This was the poster used by the Conservatives in the General Election of 30 May

1929, when they lost to Labour: Miss Brodie's jibe that Baldwin had 'got in as Prime Minister and got out again ere long' presumably refers to his first, brief, spell as P.M. from May 1923 till January 1924, rather than to his much longer period in office from November 1924 till the 1929 election. Muriel Spark can hardly expect her readers to know all these details, but it is clear that she herself does, and the sense of an accurate, detailed knowledge of the 'world' of the book is a central part of its effect.

Between Two Wars

Such details of the political life of the time help suggest the particulars of the period, but Spark creates the sense of period by larger gestures, as well. Above all, it was a time between two great wars. The first is quickly established as a relevant presence in the lives of these characters by the prominence given to the story of Miss Brodie's fiancé, slain 'the week before Armistice was declared' (12). This private tragedy is fitted in to a more general pattern of the time a little later in the novel when Jean Brodie is discussed as typical of a whole generation of women whose lives have been maimed in exactly this way – women in a state of 'war-bereaved spinsterhood' (42). As for the other end of the period, a reminder – if one is necessary – of what lay ahead for this generation of young people is planted in the novel almost as quickly – at the opening of the second chapter, in the description of Mary MacGregor's death while on leave from the Wrens during the Second World War.

It seems at first a curious decision, though, to have poor Mary slain not as a result of enemy action but in such domestic, accidental circumstances, even though she is in uniform while a world war is going on. This death, however, is similar to the even more decisive death of Joyce Emily Hammond – who is also enrolled in a violent conflict but is also killed on its fringes, accidentally, as it were. It is as if Muriel Spark wishes us to recall just how violent and desperate these times were, but also wishes to underline how, even in times of great evil, the fate of each individual is, in a way, an accident, and cannot always be directly linked to that evil. Indeed, looking at the book as a whole, it is striking how little impact Hitler's war as such seems to have on the lives of these characters: it kills none of them, and hardly seems to divert their lives from their courses. As I say, the war is something we are very aware of as we read – we automatically think of the period in which the schoolgirls are in school as 'pre-war' – but its lack of any obvious importance in plot terms is striking.

Nevertheless, even without such specific references to the warfare which closed the decade, we cannot read all the references to Mussolini and his fascisti, and the later ones to Hitler and his similar movement in Germany, without knowing perfectly well where all that is going to lead. The sense of a period which ended in a terrible war is very strong throughout the novel: all Muriel Spark needs to do is to evoke the Thirties, and our knowledge of the time will conjure up the war to come. She hardly needs to mention it directly, and it is explicitly referred to only occasionally, and in the most casual, natural way.

Life in the 1930s

If the existence of Hitler and Mussolini is the clearest indication of the Thirties, there are plenty of other reminders of the period. The other great issue which dominated those days, apart from the international situation, was the economic one: it was a time of great recession, with unemployment as the chief social ill which came about as a result. The collapse of the New York Stock Market in 1929 started a world-wide economic crisis which was at its worst in the first few years of the Thirties decade and from which the world only slowly and with difficulty recovered. Thus, the schoolgirls are glimpsing the immediate results of that collapse when, in March 1931, they are taken on their walk through the Old Town of Edinburgh, and see for the first time the destitution from which they had been sheltered in their middle-class security (27–41).

Furthermore, Spark adds a multitude of details which accurately reflect the world of the Thirties – it is in the little things, so often, that the distinctiveness of a period is to be found. These details are largely found in the first third of the book, where they can do their work of establishing a sense of period before the main action of the novel really begins to build up. Thus, the pages at the beginning of the third chapter (42–43), in which the narrator paints a general picture of the class of Edinburgh lady to which Jean Brodie belongs, is a detailed evocation of a very precise time – and a very precise place, as we find in the reference to 'Professor Tovey's Sunday Concerts' (43). (Donald Francis Tovey was Professor of Music at Edinburgh University during the 20s and 30s, and gave frequent piano recitals and orchestral concerts in the Usher Hall on Sunday afternoons, which were popular with the intelligentsia and the middle-classes.) An even briefer detail – very much of the period – has a hidden reference to the idea of the changes that time brings in people's lives – which is one of the themes of the novel: 'Sandy's mother had a flashy winter coat trimmed with fluffy fox fur like the Duchess of York's' (18). Six years later, in 1936, the Duchess of York would unexpectedly find herself Queen of Great Britain when her husband became George VI after his brother Edward stepped down from the throne in the abdication crisis: the new king and queen already had two daughters, one of whom is the present queen. The Duchess of York is now Queen Elizabeth, the Queen Mother. This reference to her earlier title is one of the multitude of ways in which the novel creates a sense of 'then and now'.

Jean Brodie and Fascism

Within all the minute details through which the Thirties are sketched in the novel, however, the most persistent and systematic element is the stream of references to the rise of Mussolini and Hitler: the growing and shifting public awareness of these increasingly threatening overseas figures can be glimpsed in the little comments Jean Brodie makes about the countries in which she spends her summer holidays, until, by 1938, Fascism is perceived as a dangerous creed not to be tolerated in British society – hence its usefulness to Miss Mackay as a charge against Miss Brodie. 'She's a born Fascist' (125). So persistent are these references, and so important is the idea of fascism in the outcome of the novel, that one is tempted to see the novel as being, in some sense, 'about' fascism.

What is fascism? It is the system of government which first emerged in Italy in 1922, in which the State and its apparatus assume complete and unchallengeable control over the individual. Fascist regimes also tend to be nationalistic, right-wing, and violently anti-communist, but the essential feature is the idea that the State is supreme and that all alternative points of view, whether held by individuals or by individual groups (such as trades unions) cannot be tolerated. A country under a fascist regime is essentially put on a war footing (whether it is at war or not – but there is a tendency for fascist regimes to be war-mongering to help justify their behaviour), and a ruling party, usually dominated by a dictator, uses all means to root out all opposition.

In more liberal regimes, the underlying assumption tends to be that the State is organised for the benefit of the individual and individuality, and that politics should be organised so as to allow for a free interchange of different points of view. The term 'fascism' comes from the Italian 'fascio', 'a bundle', and suggests the strength of a single, close unity in which the individual is subordinate to the State. Mussolini's Italy, from 1922 onwards, provided the model, and it was followed by similar regimes in Germany under Hitler and his Nazis, in Spain under General Franco, who was victorious in the Spanish Civil War (1936–39), and in several other European countries during the Thirties.

In what sense, therefore, could Jean Brodie reasonably be called 'a born Fascist'? She is clearly an admirer of Hitler and Mussolini. She is attracted by their apparent ability to organise their countries – countries which, in the years immediately after the First World War, had been variously stricken, demoralised, and politically divided, and which, furthermore, were suffering as much as anywhere from the economic troubles of the age. She is drawn to the imagery of fascism – to the military uniforms, to the outward improvements fascism allegedly brought about, like the banishment of litter from the streets (31) and – no doubt – like Mussolini's famous achievement of making the Italian trains run on time. She favours Franco rather than the Republicans in Spain, and urges Joyce Emily Hammond to fight on his side, rather than on the side for which her brother, like thousands of other idealistic young men of liberal or leftish sympathies, is fighting. (Joyce is killed, of course, when her train is attacked, even before she reaches the fighting.) After the Second World War Jean Brodie's judgement is merely that 'Hitler *was* rather naughty' (122).

Nevertheless, Jean Brodie is not really interested in politics, as Sandy Stranger admits to Miss Mackay (125). She sees in fascism only what she wants to see, and what she likes about it is its style – it transforms the appearance of a country into order and uniformity, and lays great stress on public displays of virile, marching men. Sandy is quite right: Miss Brodie is not interested in the politics of fascism. It is one of the striking things about her that in that intensely politically-aware decade she seems to be completely without any political instincts. When she rejects Stanley Baldwin and his boring political message, she does so in philosophical, rather than political terms: 'Safety does not come first. Goodness, Truth and Beauty come first. Follow me.' (10)

This little incident illustrates, however, Jean Brodie's

blindness and also the tendency of the whole novel to suggest broad implications within apparently slight and superficial details. Jean Brodie rejects Baldwin for his superficial and unglamorous approach to living; she declares for values of ultimate importance. Then: 'Follow me.' This is apparently just the teacher's command to get a halted line of pupils moving again. It is hard, however, to avoid seeing it also as an expression of Jean Brodie's unconscious appeal to the children to choose her and her glamorous style rather than Baldwin and his prudence. 'Follow me.' Baldwin's campaign message shows how a life style (as we'd now call it) can be used as a political weapon. The teacher's reply to Baldwin also has the power to influence 'political' matters – both in the narrow political arena of the power-struggle going on in the school, and also in the great European struggle which gathered momentum during the 1930s: Joyce Emily Hammond goes off to Spain inspired by her teacher. 'Follow me' are words which automatically set up their speaker as a leader and in 'Safety does not come first, et cetera' Jean Brodie is asking the girls to choose her as their leader rather than people who are more boring. She is offering them a style of leadership, glamorous, daring, in touch with deep truths, capable of leading followers from a depressing present to a glorious future. In her small way, she is offering what Mussolini and Hitler offered to their depressed post-war nations. She has a little of their charisma which welded followers into unified masses. Mussolini swayed the Italians as their 'Duce'; Hitler dominated the Germans as their 'Fuehrer'. Both words mean 'leader'; both men essentially said to their countrymen, 'Follow me.'

Used strictly, the term 'fascist' is meaningless if it does *not* refer to a concept of how a state should be organised: fascism is all about the politics of a nation, or it is about nothing. Muriel Spark, however, seems to be willing to use the word in a much more general kind of way, to refer to an individual's habit of mind and personality: 'By now, [Sandy] had entered the Catholic Church, in whose ranks she had found quite a number of Fascists much less agreeable than Miss Brodie' (125). Here, the term is being used to describe people who do not tolerate views other than their own, and who are unscrupulous in their methods of gaining control over the minds and behaviour of other people. The word is regularly used, nowadays, to refer to anyone who seems to be ruthlessly rooting out ideological opposition, though normally there are political issues involved. (This occurs when, for example, the police are abused as 'Fascists' if they break up demonstrations during industrial disputes.) In the 'betrayal' of Jean Brodie, however, no such political dimension exists, as Sandy admits. Thus it is, in a sense, a trumped-up charge when Miss Brodie is forced to retire 'on the grounds that she had been teaching Fascism' (125). There had been no political content in what she had been teaching – no attempt, for example, to further the cause of the British Fascists (of whom there were quite a number, followers of the charismatic politician Sir Oswald Mosley – whose movement, strangely, is never mentioned in the course of the novel). She had expressed admiration for Italy's vigorous Fascisti, just as she had expressed admiration for Italy's painters, and for Italy's Dante, and for Italy's way of pronouncing the name Beatrice (46). When Sandy later says that Miss Brodie 'was quite an innocent in her way' (127) she is apparently saying that Miss Brodie lacked a lot of knowledge about our sinful world, but she is also very near saying – and perhaps she is saying (or thinking, at least) – that Miss Brodie 'was innocent', i.e. had been accused and convicted of something which she had not done.

Jean Brodie and Hitler

When one first begins to think about the novel, there is a strong temptation to see it as showing that dangerous fascist instincts can lurk in the most unlikely places – here, within the bosom of an obscure Edinburgh spinster schoolmistress. The strange charge which is finally brought against her seems, if anything, to be confirmed when one looks at the parallels between Jean Brodie and the greatest (or worst!) fascist of the day. Her dates are 1890–1946; Hitler's are 1889–1945. They both die round about the age of fifty-six. Miss Brodie's 'prime' starts in 1930, around the time when Sandy's class first encounters her (11) – presumably in late August when the Scottish school year normally starts. Meanwhile, Hitler and his Nazis had their first major political success in the German election of September 1930, in which they became the second largest political party in the German Parliament, having been the smallest of nine parties before the election. This was their big breakthrough, and they burst into influence just when Miss Brodie was first bursting upon the little girls of the story.

One's natural suspicion that Muriel Spark was not thinking in this kind of way when she was writing the book, and that this parallel is probably coincidence, takes a bit of a knock when one considers the timing of the event which puts a stop to Miss Brodie's prime: the 'betrayal' by Sandy. This clearly takes place in the autumn of 1938 (124) and so occurs within weeks of the infamous Munich Agreement of 29 September 1938 which resulted in the handing over of much of Czechoslovakia to Germany – a decision which is generally regarded as a betrayal of the Czechs. And Miss Brodie's constant whine, at the end of her life, about her betrayal seems a further possible echo of Hitler, who ended his days in his bunker in Berlin, denouncing all those who had betrayed him.

So is Jean Brodie a kind of Hitler? This is a crude way of expressing what seems to be Sandy's view of her at the moment of 'betrayal'. Not only does she seem to Sandy to be a fascist – this is how Sandy has tended to think of her ever since the walk through Edinburgh back in 1931 – but she is also capable, apparently, of causing someone's death, as the fate of Joyce Emily Hammond seems to suggest. There are difficulties with this line of thought, however. For one thing, whoever was betrayed at Munich, it was not Hitler, and so the attempt to read the Brodie betrayal as a close parallel of the simultaneous international events falls down. Poor Miss Brodie is indeed 'put a stop to', but Munich is significant as being the moment when, maybe, Britain and France had a chance to put a stop to Hitler, but did not take it.

If anything, Sandy's behaviour in betraying Miss Brodie to the authorities – on a somewhat trumped-up charge – echoes a rather different feature of National Socialism: the way in which children, indoctrinated in Nazi ideology, would sometimes betray their parents to the Nazi authorities. The relationship between Jean Brodie and her 'set' has clear suggestions of a parent-child relationship: the girls are, in some sense, substitutes for the offspring she never had, and Sandy, at least, has a relationship with her which goes beyond that of pupil and teacher. The sense that we all feel that, in betraying Miss Brodie, Sandy is doing something shocking derives, I think, from this aspect of the book.

The nearest, perhaps, that we can safely go in using the parallel with Munich to interpret the betrayal by Sandy is to say that treachery and betrayal seem to be in the air around this time. Yet both betrayals are decisive, each in its sphere and just as Miss Brodie is decisively destroyed in a meeting at which she is not present, so the Czechs were shamefully excluded from the decisive meetings between Hitler on the one hand and the prime ministers of Britain, France and Italy on the other, meetings which handed over a third of Czechoslovakia to Germany and left her defenceless. For a while, the Munich agreement could seem to many to be less an act of treachery than a wise and welcome act of statesmanship. Neville Chamberlain claimed that he had gained 'peace for our time... peace with honour'. It is mainly in retrospect that it seems both wrong and futile. Similarly, Sandy seems to have, in Joyce Emily Hammond's death, a sufficient immediate cause for her act of personal treachery. In the longer perspective, however, it seems far less certain that the teacher has been fairly dealt with. This is to raise, however, the question of the rights and wrongs of these characters and their actions, a matter about which it is particularly difficult to come to a simple conclusion.

RELIGION IN THE NOVEL

Sandy's Conversion

Most of the novel is set in and around Edinburgh during the 1930s. It ends, however, in an unnamed convent, located (vaguely) 'deep in the country' (127), with Sandy receiving one of a steady stream of visitors who wish to talk to her as a famous author, or as an old friend with whom they can reminisce and who provides them with 'a spiritual sensation' (121). Looked at one way, the novel tells the story of Jean Brodie and her betrayal; looked at another way, it tells the story of how an Edinburgh schoolgirl becomes a nun. Religion is one of the important aspects of the novel. Indeed, we might say that it provides a framework within which these characters live their lives and that it is a framework constructed out of two religious traditions which Spark regards as very different, Calvinism and Catholicism. Catholicism is a clear-cut religious denomination, of course, but Calvinism is a powerful strand of religious thought which cuts across denominational boundaries. In Scotland, however, they tend to have been long viewed as polar opposites: the main post-Reformation religious tradition in Scotland has been Calvinist, and Catholicism was, for generations of Scottish church-goers, the ultimate anathema which they were rejecting.

Sandy becomes a Roman Catholic, which is the religion to which Muriel Spark was converted in 1954. Like so much else in this brief and flowing novel, the inner process by which Sandy makes this crucial decision in her life is not depicted in any detail or at any length. Here is the relevant passage, which follows on from the account of how Sandy and Teddy Lloyd have an affair, even though he is still obsessed with Jean Brodie:

> The more she discovered him to be still in love with Jean Brodie, the more she was curious about the mind that loved the woman. By the end of the year it happened that she had quite lost interest in the man himself, but was deeply absorbed in his mind, from which she extracted, among other things, his religion as a pith from a husk. Her mind was as full of his religion as a night sky is full of things visible and invisible. She left the man and took his religion and became a nun in the course of time. (123)

This seems a most unusual route to religious belief. Finding, in the course of an adulterous affair, that her partner is still really in love with someone else, Sandy does not react as a jealous rival but instead detaches herself, investigating what is involved when one person, against all reason, loves another. This interest in the workings of the human mind is something of which Sandy has shown signs before but it is clearly developing greatly under the pressure of this first adult situation in which she finds herself. Yet her investigation leads not just to a deeper understanding of human psychology, but also to a sudden religious commitment. It is as if she stumbles on the right religion for her, and she is suddenly, completely, and mysteriously overwhelmed by it. We have also seen already, however, how Sandy has been developing an interest in religion: from the age of fifteen, she has been in the habit of thinking about the religious traditions of her native Edinburgh, prompted by the medieval buildings still standing in the High Street (108–109).

What is striking about this conclusion of Sandy's life, however, is that it is offered to us readers with no strong sense that a soul has been saved, or an important decision rightly taken – as we might have expected, considering Spark's own Catholicism. Sandy's religious destination provides no resounding, positive conclusion: it is always mentioned in a purely matter-of-fact way. If anything, there is something rather troubling about the picture we have of Sandy as a nun:

> She clutched the bars of the grille as if she wanted to escape from the dim parlour beyond, for she was not composed like the other nuns who sat, when they received their rare visitors, well back in the darkness with folded hands. But Sandy always leaned forward and peered, clutching the bars with both hands, and the other sisters remarked it and said that Sister Helena had too much to bear from the world since she had published her psychological book which was so unexpectedly famed. But the dispensation was forced upon Sandy ... .(35)

Sandy's decision to become a nun suggests an impulse, on her part, to retreat from the world yet her behaviour with visitors suggests a desire 'to escape from the dim parlour beyond' – back into the world; the meetings with visitors seem, however, to be 'forced upon Sandy' by the church authorities. She is clearly in a pitiable state of tension, but does she want to be completely out of the world, or back into it? I don't think that there is a clear or simple answer to this: we are given too little information about Sandy's life as a nun. In a book which has so fully analysed other aspects of the central characters, this is clearly deliberate, and a degree of puzzlement seems to be Spark's intention.

Yet some things can be said. The state of being completely caught between, on the one hand, devotion to God and, on the other, entanglement with the world seems to be the point. Furthermore, it seems clear that we should believe that there is a connection between Sandy's fate and the fact that she has been influenced by Jean Brodie. The book closes with the repetition of Sandy's answer to the inquisitive young man:

> 'What were the main influences of your school days, Sister Helena? Were they literary or political or personal? Was it Calvinism?'
> Sandy said: 'There was a Miss Jean Brodie in her prime.' (128)

This means nothing to him, of course, but it is clearly meant to be thoroughly meaningful for us. When this conversation is first reported to us, it is given in a slightly fuller, more helpful guise:

> 'The influences of one's teens are very important,' said the man.
> 'Oh yes,' said Sandy, 'even if they provide something to react against.'
> 'What was your biggest influence, then, Sister Helena? Was it political, personal? Was it Calvinism?'
> 'Oh no,' said Sandy. 'But there was a Miss Jean Brodie in her prime.' (34–35)

At first glance, the differences between these two versions of the conversation seem insignificant. When one stops to think of it, though, it seems slightly odd that there should be any differences at all: Spark as author is presumably imagining a tale with the apparent solidity of real life, and has gone to great lengths in other matters – in the business of dates, for example – to achieve that effect. Yet each of these versions sits on the page as if it alone were the accurate transcript of what was said. Why does she not exactly repeat the first version to maintain that effect? They can't, as it were, both be right.

I think that she means to suggest two different implications. In the first, fuller version, Sandy's reply is a denial of the

suggestions made by the young man, and Jean Brodie is mentioned as an alternative influence instead – i.e. an influence which
was not political, or personal, or Calvinism. 'Oh no. But there was
a Miss Jean Brodie in her prime.' The second version, at the end
of the book, is far less clearly a denial of the alternatives put to
her. In fact, it could even be read as summing up literary, political,
personal and Calvinistic influences in the person of the
mysterious Miss Jean Brodie. The first version offers us some
superficial alternatives; the second takes us, in its brevity and
simplicity, to the heart of the matter.

What can we make of this? Thinking about both versions, and
about the whole book as well, we can perhaps see that what is
being implied is that the things the young man suggests had no
decisive influence *in themselves* even though they were part of
Sandy's life, but that because they were embodied in Jean Brodie
they became part of the teacher's influence. Jean Brodie was the
real influence, not these abstract things, but they gained an
influence through her and contributed to her total effect on Sandy.
Without her, the abstractions would have had no clear influence;
in her, they did.

Jean Brodie as Justified Sinner

Yet it still seems strange to be thinking about Jean Brodie in a
religious way at all: she does not obviously appear to be a figure of
religious significance. It is true that she goes to church – indeed,
she goes to various churches so long as they are not Roman
Catholic (85). This account of her church-going, however, quickly
develops into a discussion of her attitudes to right and wrong,
attitudes which seem to have a great bearing on the book as a
whole.

> She was not in any doubt, she let everyone know she
> was in no doubt, that God was on her side whatever
> her course, and so she experienced no difficulty or
> sense of hypocrisy in worship while at the same time
> she went to bed with the singing master. Just as an
> excessive sense of guilt can drive people to excessive
> action, so was Miss Brodie driven to it by an
> excessive lack of guilt.

This is the kind of topic to which the book returns a little later, at
the point at which Sandy is described responding to the Calvinist

traditions of Edinburgh, and sensing there the age-old belief in an Old Testament god who delights in hellfire and punishment, and who was thought to have destined for eternal damnation the great majority of the human beings whom he had created. When Miss Gaunt and the Kerr sisters are described as believing 'that God had planned for practically everybody before they were born a nasty surprise when they died' (108), the reference is to the central Calvinist belief that not only is there a hell to which some human beings will go, and that in fact the large majority of mankind will end up there, but also that God must have planned who would go and who wouldn't because God, being all-powerful and willing everything that happens everywhere even down to the tiniest detail, must have planned all the details of that crucial matter, as well. So (goes the line of argument), God, who created Time and who is therefore outside Time, must have decided who would go to Heaven and who would go to Hell even before there were any people (or Time) at all – before the Creation.

The key idea in this kind of thought is the notion that everything which happens has been planned by God so that everything – absolutely everything – is God's will. But if God has made *all* the decisions, right down to my going off for a cup of coffee at this point as I write, then I am not making any real decision for myself – I have no choice, in a sense, but to go off for the coffee. If I decide, at the very last minute, to skip the coffee, I still haven't made any decision for myself: I've still just acted out God's will which turns out to be different from what I'd expected. God's will can't be thwarted; it can only be misunderstood.

This kind of thinking removes any notion of free will in human behaviour. If this is a true notion of God, then we can't claim the credit for the good things we do, because really God has willed them, not us. Similarly, however, one might argue that we can't be blamed for the bad things we do, either: in performing them, we are still carrying out the divine will. Now, it is obviously rather hard – probably impossible – to know for certain that all this is really true of the relationship between God and ourselves, just as it is really impossible for anyone to be sure that he or she has been chosen by God to go to Heaven rather than to Hell. Most people (and, in particular, most Christians) are sensible enough to realise that these are matters about which we can't really be certain.

In particular, most Christians, even when they are Calvinists, have realised that we can't know for a fact that God has chosen us to be saved, and that salvation is so sure and certain that it doesn't matter what we do on earth. But, there have occasionally been people who *did* believe that they were so chosen by God, and that whatever they did had been preordained and (as it were) sanctioned by God so that the perpetration of wrongs, and even of crimes, would make no difference. An earlier Scottish writer, James Hogg (1770–1835) once wrote a famous novel, *The Private Memoirs and Confessions of a Justified Sinner*, about just such a character, an unfortunate young man called Robert Wringhim. (There is a *Scotnote* about this book, by Elaine Petrie.)

So, when we are told that Jean Brodie 'was not in any doubt ... that God was on her side whatever her course', we know that we are here dealing with another character like the one in Hogg's novel. There is not so much direct theology in Spark's book as there is in Hogg's, but the end result is the same: both are about characters who feel disastrously certain about too much – about everything important in their lives, in fact. Like Hogg's Robert Wringhim, Jean Brodie feels free to write her own rules and to begin to intervene in the lives of others (Wringhim intervenes to the extent of committing murder, and one might argue that in encouraging Joyce Emily Hammond to set off to Spain Jean Brodie is beginning to go to similar lengths).

In big things and in small, Jean Brodie rates her own ideas, views and preferences as if they were what God himself thinks, so that it is apparently enough for Giotto to be *her* favourite Italian painter for her to be able to insist that he was also the *greatest* one (11). Her thought and speech is a cascade of opinions and beliefs which often strike us as dotty but about which she has not the shadow of a doubt. She is bossy, domineering, tyrannical, because she does not allow for the possibility of any other view but her own. At first, we just regard all this as part of her peculiar personality, but as the religious references in the book build up, we find that Spark is relating this behaviour to more fundamental levels of right and wrong. Jean Brodie's story is the story of someone who comes to disaster as a result of a false and foolish certainty. She does not suspect that she might be wrong, either in understanding or in behaviour. She has 'an excessive lack of guilt' (85).

On the personal level, Sandy reacts against Jean Brodie; on the religious level, Sandy reacts against the Calvinist spirit which is expressed in her native Edinburgh and becomes a very different kind of Christian, a Catholic. Jean Brodie is rather anti-Catholic and is clearly, to some extent, a product of Edinburgh (or Scottish) Calvinism. The kind of disastrous theological mistake which Robert Wringhim and (more instinctively) Jean Brodie make is one to which Protestant believers are perhaps more prone than Catholics. Catholicism values the teaching authority of the Church and lays much stress on the power of those above (bishops and popes) when it comes to matters of belief; Protestantism lays greater stress on the beliefs which well up naturally within each individual believer. Thus it is probably easier for a Protestant, thinking and feeling in essential isolation, to develop an individualistic (and quirkily excessive) notion about right and wrong, salvation and damnation, and other areas of belief. Jean Brodie may not be an obviously religious figure, but it is perfectly possible to interpret her behaviour in religious terms and Muriel Spark has included enough of a religious context in the book for that to happen. Typical of her Edinburgh origins in so many ways, Jean Brodie distils the Calvinist traditions of the place to an excessive and dangerous extent.

Sandy and Catholicism

Sandy's Catholicism is presented, both implicitly and explicitly, as a reaction against the Calvinist Miss Brodie. The book does not touch on the nature of Catholicism to quite the same extent as it treats the nature of Calvinism: it is mainly present in the book as a very different religion, merely. If Calvinism, as Muriel Spark views it here, has within it the potential to release such dangerously self-assured individuals as Wringhim and Miss Brodie, fuelled and isolated by their private certainties, so at least part of the virtue of Spark's Catholicism seems to reside in its ability to subordinate individualistic impulses. This is perhaps linked partly to its authoritarian tradition but also to its stress on the harmonious relatedness of all things, its insistence that there is pattern and meaning behind all the seemingly chaotic circumstances of life.

Miss Brodie's notion that Catholicism is a religion for people 'who did not want to think for themselves' (85) is thoroughly disproved by Sandy, at least, for it is as a Catholic that she writes 'her odd psychological treatise on the nature of moral perception' (35), which in its oddness and in its fame is clearly the product of someone very much thinking for herself. Yet it has to be admitted that Sandy does not seem to be a very comfortable Catholic, even though we are given no grounds for thinking that she will ever be in any danger of ceasing to be one. As it is presented in this novel, Catholicism seems to be capable of accommodating a very wide range of temperaments: Sandy's anguished, intellectualised truth-seeking; Teddy Lloyd's simple, spontaneous sinning; possibly even Jean Brodie's 'soaring and diving spirit' (85). The Calvinist Church of Scotland ejects Gordon Lowther because of his affair with Jean Brodie, but there seems to be no such incompatibility between Catholic sinners (like Teddy Lloyd) and their church. It isn't that Catholicism condones sin; however, it seems capable of coming to terms with sinners in a way that, in this book at least, the Calvinist church cannot. We naturally wonder, however, why Sandy seems to be such a tormented Catholic and the probable answer, as so often in this book, surely lies in Jean Brodie's influence. The teacher has developed Sandy's capacity for striking, individualistic action, and has herself become the main victim of that capacity. The source of Sandy's discontents in her religious vocation probably lies here: it is as if Sandy has adopted an eternal strait-jacket for the safety of others and also of herself.

Despite all this, it is not, strictly speaking, a religious novel: it does not narrowly explore any character's religious experience; it does not set out to weigh the merits of one creed against another; it does not attempt to communicate anything of divine mystery. Yet religion is an important part of it, because religion is an important, indeed inescapable, part of Muriel Spark's sense of the world. As we have seen, it does not seem to have been an accident that Mrs Spark started writing novels so soon after she became a Catholic: her Catholic belief seems to have put her in the position, suddenly, of being able to write the kind of novels she was born to write. What it gave her, apparently, was a sense of something absolute, fixed, morally certain, in comparison with which all human ideas and standards appear shifting, not final. She put it this way:

> I'm quite certain that my conversion gave me something to work on as a satirist. The Catholic belief is a norm from which one can depart. It's not a fluctuating thing.

A satirist is a writer who mocks or criticises imperfect behaviour and consequently needs some notion of what is perfect in order to be able to make the criticism. Most of Muriel Spark's novels are wittily amused depictions of human folly and imperfection and even when they contain still less in the way of explicit religious references than *The Prime of Miss Jean Brodie* does, one can readily believe that they have been written with a sense that there are absolute standards of right and wrong, wisdom and folly. Not, however, any old standards of right and wrong, wisdom and folly: that is precisely Jean Brodie's mistake. She sets up as final her own idiosyncratic notions of value: the result is often comic but it leads to tragedy.

ASSESSING JEAN BRODIE

What Are We to Make of Her?

If it is harder to be certain about what is good and valuable than Jean Brodie seems to think, it is also surprisingly hard for the reader to be certain about whether or not Jean Brodie herself is good and valuable. If we imply, as I have done in the previous section, that she has practically set herself up as God, then it sounds as if she is being at best pitied by Muriel Spark, and at worst deplored. There seems to be plenty of cause for regarding Jean Brodie as the villain of the piece, a view that would appear to receive its final confirmation in the decisive way in which Sandy betrays her former teacher and engineers her removal from the school. What prompts this action, of course, is the revelation of how Miss Brodie has meddled in the business of Joyce Emily Hammond going off to the war in Spain, but the teacher's behaviour in this matter is not really different from her character-istic behaviour throughout the book: it is only that the stakes (life and death) are higher. Almost as astonishing is the way in which Jean Brodie tries to organise the love-lives of her former pupils. But then, she has always tried to organise the preferences, views, and futures of her favourite pupils, in matters great and small. This, in turn, is clearly tied up with her habitual bossiness and selfishness, illustrated right at the beginning as she comes out at the school gate and disengages the groups of girls and boys who are naturally, and rightly, starting to initiate relationships with each other.

But if Jean Brodie's unceasing attempt to mould what her girls will become can seem, on some pages, to be merely the behaviour of an intolerably domineering nature, at other times it can seem to be the creditable activity of an unorthodox but gifted teacher. When we first hear of the unexpected things about which her young pupils have been informed (the Buchmanites and Mussolini, cleansing cream and witch-hazel, *et cetera*) do we not have a favourable response? Are we not pleased to catch a whiff of teaching which is obviously vigorous, imaginative and tending to open up to young girls a stimulating sense of the fascinating and bewildering complexities of real life? The first impression we have of Jean Brodie is of a teacher who is independent of the predictable confines of a syllabus – and that must surely be a positive impression? 'How sensible!' we think to ourselves, and wish that all our teachers had been like that.

It is true that our favourable response to her educational efforts is sometimes mixed with disapproval. For example, Miss Brodie is unattractively intolerant of Eunice who prefers to go to a church social rather than take a once-in-a-lifetime chance to see the great ballerina Anna Pavlova perform (62), and it is while the girls are being marched on their walk through Edinburgh that Sandy discovers the idea that Miss Brodie has moulded them into her own fascisti (31–32). Such expeditions, to some extent, express Brodie the tyrant. Yet they are also genuinely enlarging: to see Pavlova is an opportunity worth taking, and Jean Brodie is the only person offering the chance to the girls. The walk through Edinburgh is partly an uncomfortable experience for Sandy and the others, but it is also extremely revealing and memorable for them (as its prominence in Chapter Two suggests). Miss Brodie is clearly capable of opening up the world to these girls as no other adult they are encountering can do.

Compared with the rest of the school staff, Jean Brodie seems to be a very good thing indeed. In comparison with her, all the other female teachers seem to be either anonymous and unimaginative upholders of traditional and anti-individualistic values, or else narrow, warped individuals. Miss Lockhart, the science teacher whom Gordon Lowther eventually marries, lives with the potential to do something imaginative and drastic (blow up the school with her gunpowder) but would never dream of doing so (114), and she lives in a classroom world of certainties (the simple experiments are all foregone conclusions) and familiar unspontaneous routine (she always teaches her classes in the same way). Miss Mackay, the headmistress, is a dogged defender of tried and respectable methods of teaching: her only distinction is her unremitting antipathy to Jean Brodie. She talks sturdy common sense (as in the matter of the girls' choice of Classical or Modern courses, for example) but she entirely lacks any charisma.

And if her female colleagues cannot compete with Miss Brodie in terms of liveliness and spontaneity as a teacher, they equally cannot compete with her in terms of sex-appeal, as the responses of the two men on the staff, Teddy Lloyd and Gordon Lowther, make abundantly clear. Lowther eventually marries Miss Lockhart, who is less passionate and more normally companionable than the intense Miss Brodie; he is really rather bourgeois and humdrum himself, but Jean Brodie has shaken him, for a while at least, out of the confines of respectable behaviour. Lloyd, the artist with more than a touch of the bohemian in him, remains adulterously besotted with Jean Brodie even when he is having affairs with other people. For both of these men, she is an intensely enlivening presence.

What Do Other Characters Make of Her?

Judgements such as these depend on our trying to pick up the implications of the events of the book; they are far from being explicitly stated there. It is natural, however, to look for some more explicit judgement on Jean Brodie from the other characters: any such statement, one might think, ought to take us a little nearer the author's own conception. Yet no other character sums up Jean Brodie in a way which seems authoritative. The conversations on the last two pages of the book revolve round various assessments of her but none seems conclusive. Eunice looks back on her warmly: she puts flowers on the grave and remembers her old teacher as 'marvellous fun'. Jenny's account of her latest experience leads her, swiftly and apparently automatically, to regard it in the light of what Jean Brodie would have thought of it. Monica thinks that loyalty was owed to Miss Brodie, and seems to be prodding Sandy to admit that she was the betrayer, something which she notably avoids doing. To all these girls, their old teacher, long dead, is still a presence in their lives.

Sandy's last utterances, however, seem marked by a distinctly enigmatic quality: 'Sandy replied like an enigmatic Pope ...' (126); 'Oh, she was quite an innocent in her way' (127); 'It's only possible to betray where loyalty is due. ... Only up to a point' (127); 'There was a Miss Jean Brodie in her prime' (128). She is speaking the truth, but in a puzzling way which conceals as much as it reveals. We feel that of all the other characters Sandy is probably the most capable of summing up Miss Brodie: she is not only the cleverest of the girls (at least in terms of having produced a markedly clever book) but also, obviously, the most spiritually alive and intense. Furthermore, her puzzling utterances seem to come as fragments of a coherent, complex but settled understanding of the nature and significance of Jean Brodie; they carry weight. As she speaks, we feel that Sandy has indeed come to a full understanding of Jean Brodie, and of the events in which they had all been involved. Nevertheless, while the last sentence of the book does acknowledge, with the utmost weight, the decisive influence of the teacher, the very simplicity and decisiveness of the acknowledgement avoids any implication about whether that influence was for good or bad. The book ends on an assertion of fact, but an avoidance of judgement. There is a sense of a secure, adequate judgement, not only possible but actually achieved by Sandy. Yet she does not ever give it full expression, and we do not know whether this is because it is so complex that words cannot adequately convey it, or because Sandy feels that none of her hearers could properly understand all its nuances, or because she does not consider it sufficiently important to try to express it. Sandy conveys a sense of a religious perspective on Jean Brodie, a perspective which has the air of being more true and adequate than any other view of her. Yet the very existence of that perspective seems to depend on its not being fully put into words: it just exists, and we can glimpse only little bits of it.

Sandy's final, mysterious understanding of Jean Brodie can casually include contradictions:

> 'Miss Brodie would have liked to know about it,'
> [Jenny] said, 'sinner as she was.'
> 'Oh, she was quite an innocent in her way,' said
> Sandy. (127)

Judges less confident and penetrating than the mature Sandy, like Jenny or the reader, are liable to find the contradictions a little more bewildering than Sandy does. Whatever we say or think in judgement of Jean Brodie, some opposite consideration comes swiftly to mind, as if to contradict it. She was a stimulating, unorthodox teacher? Yes, but in many ways she is the absolute embodiment of a conventional old-style Scottish spinster schoolmistress, full of petty rules and facts which the pupils find rather meaningless but which they have to try to remember. She embodies higher artistic and moral ideals than most of those around her? Yes, but her utterances about the great things of art and life are thrown out willy-nilly and mixed up with all kinds of petty detail in a completely indiscriminate way. Does she *really* appreciate the great things in life, we wonder?:

> Here is a Cimabue. [Cimabue was a 13th-century
> Italian painter.] Here is a larger formation of
> Mussolini's fascisti, it is a better view of them than
> that of last year's picture. They are doing splendid

> things as I shall tell you later. I went with my
> friends for an audience with the Pope. My friends
> kissed his ring but I thought it proper only to bend
> over it. I wore a long black gown with a lace
> mantilla, and looked magnificent. ... (44)

She devotes herself selflessly to the education of her girls, denying
herself the distraction of marriage? That is what it looks like from
the outside, but the reality is that she can't have the man she
really loves (Teddy Lloyd) because he is married already, and uses
her girls as an extension of her own personality, even trying to
organise some of them into bed with him. Her educational
approach has a decisive influence on the girls? It is true that her
memory remains with them for the rest of their lives and that
Sandy seems to have been influenced by her more profoundly. For
most of them, however, her influence is something which they
shrug off in the few years after leaving her. There is no visible
pattern to their later lives: they seem to become what they
become, despite her.

Brodies, Old and New

She is a figure of contradictions, an assessment which is confirmed, it would seem, by the implications of her name. In a
rather unexpected passage, she claims descent from the famous
Deacon Brodie, prominent eighteenth-century Edinburgh citizen
by day and successful burglar by night (88). He is frequently
regarded as a particularly clear embodiment of the human tendency to have an open, virtuous public side, and also a hidden,
dark, private aspect. We don't know, of course, whether or not to
take seriously this claim that Deacon Brodie was an ancestor of
hers, yet Spark seems to wish us to accept that there is at least a
measure of spiritual kinship between the two Brodies. This
reference to Deacon Brodie is not the first time he has been used
in literature: it is well known that Robert Louis Stevenson was
fascinated by him and at one point he helped write a play about
him: *Deacon Brodie, or, The Double Life*. Stevenson's sense of the
contradictions within each of us (a theme which recurs throughout
his writings and which he expressed most memorably of all in the
work which gave him his first real success, *The Strange Case of Dr
Jekyll and Mr Hyde*) was greatly shaped by the tale of Brodie's
double life: outward, day-time respectability and hidden, night-
time, excitingly perverse wrong-doing.

> I am a descendant, do not forget, of Willie Brodie, a
> man of substance, a cabinet maker and designer of
> gibbets, a member of the Town Council of Edinburgh
> and a keeper of two mistresses who bore him five
> children between them. Blood tells. He played much
> dice and fighting cocks. Eventually he was a wanted
> man for having robbed the Excise Office – not that
> he needed the money, he was a night burglar only for
> sake of the danger in it. Of course, he was arrested
> abroad and was brought back to the Tolbooth prison,
> but that was mere chance. He died cheerfully on a
> gibbet of his own devising in seventeen-eighty-eight.
> (88)

Whereas Stevenson was drawn to the disharmonies which result
from the contradictions within such an individual, Jean Brodie
rather plays them down here, apparently less struck by Brodie's
apparent contrasts than by the sheer individualism and vigour
which the man showed. She approves of him as much for his
mistresses and illegitimate children as for his success as a
businessman and local politician. She shrugs off the moral complexity of Brodie with 'However all this may be, it is the stuff I am
made of'. We might say that she admires his style, just as, only a
few pages earlier, the girls had marvelled at Teddy Lloyd's style in
enforcing his will by the smashing of the saucer – a superficially
naughty act which compels their admiration for its extremism, its
lack of bourgeois inhibition, its focusing of individual will (79–80).
As we read Jean Brodie's account of her alleged ancestor, a
recollection of that saucer in the art room perhaps still lingers,
with the gentle references to the cups and saucers of this middle-
class teatime punctuated by Lowther's safe, conventional gestures
towards romantic boldness in his Scots songs of military glory and
tragic love-affairs. And despite her praise of Deacon Brodie's
anarchic ability to defy respectability, Jean Brodie shows herself
to be, at heart, much more thoroughly respectable than either the
earlier Brodie or even than the saucer-smashing Teddy Lloyd: she
frets over the chipped rim of a teacup.

Just as Jean Brodie plays down the deep contradictions in the
Deacon Brodie story, so she seems oblivious to the danger of her
position, despite her acknowledgement of *his* relishing of danger.
Had she taken her own parallel with Deacon Brodie more seriously, she might have survived. And this is especially true of one
important detail of the legend of Deacon Brodie which she seems
to be conveniently forgetting: disaster finally struck him when he

was betrayed by one of his own gang. Distant hints of betrayal
occur elsewhere in the book. For example, Miss Brodie's un-
compromising attitude to resignation is expressed as follows, near
the book's beginning: 'As soon expect Julius Caesar to apply for a
job at a crank school as Miss Brodie. She would never resign. If
the authorities wanted to get rid of her she would have to be
assassinated.' (9) Which, of course, is precisely what happened to
Julius Caesar, not only assassinated but famously betrayed by
Brutus his close friend: *Et tu, Brute?* It might also be relevant to
remember, as Spark may be doing here, that Shakespeare's Julius
Caesar, in the play of that name, is another of the great puzzlingly
contradictory characters of literature: a heroic titan as well as a
surprisingly limited, small-minded man.

Perhaps the Author Might Help Us?

In creating Jean Brodie, Spark is bringing home to us the
difficulty – perhaps, the impossibility – of ever finally summing
up a human being. In her central character, she has created a
strong and unique personality to which it is almost impossible to
have a lukewarm reaction. And yet there is, as we have found, a
massive difficulty in trying to come to a final and widely accept-
able assessment of her. This is a novel which has been frequently
discussed and analysed by literary critics, but there is even now,
thirty years after the book first appeared, no settled agreement
among them about whether the author seems to be essentially on
Jean Brodie's side or not – about whether she is being offered to
us as a heroine almost tragically destroyed by one of her closest
associates, or as a personality so dangerously destructive that her
betrayal comes not a moment too soon.

Great literature is usually marked by some complexity, perhaps even ambiguity, of interpretation and, at times, all readers
find themselves yearning after a decisive explanation, ideally
from the author personally. Not so easy, of course, when the
author is dead, but even when the author can be approached one's
difficulties are not necessarily solved. Very often, authors are
reticent about discussing detailed interpretations of their works
and I do not know of any instance when Muriel Spark has
commented directly and decisively on what she was trying to do in
creating the character of Jean Brodie. She has recently given us a
tantalising clue, however, in the course of that autobiographical
essay which she published in *The New Yorker* (March 25, 1991):

'Personal History: The School on the Links'. As mentioned earlier, the article is dominated, as clearly her recollections are, by one teacher in particular, Miss Christina Kay. We are told that she was a

> character in search of an author, whose classroom walls were adorned with reproductions of early and Renaissance paintings – Leonardo da Vinci, Giotto, Fra Filippo Lippi, Botticelli. She borrowed these from the senior art department, run by handsome Arthur Couling. We had the Dutch masters and Corot. Also displayed was a newspaper cutting of Mussolini's Fascisti marching along the streets of Rome.

Sounds familiar? Muriel Spark is quite open about the fact that Miss Kay was the model for Jean Brodie: 'No pupil of Miss Kay's has failed to recognize her, with joy and great nostalgia, in the shape of Miss Jean Brodie in her prime'. Moreover, it is abundantly clear from the article that Spark was, and still is, all for Miss Kay. The article is a celebration of her idiosyncratic and powerful personality; there is hardly a whiff of adverse criticism in it at all.

What we cannot do, however, is immediately leap from this back to the book and claim that the author's real feelings about the Jean Brodie character are entirely favourable. Partly this is because Spark herself distinguishes firmly between them.

> In a sense, Miss Kay was nothing like Miss Brodie. In another sense, she was far above and beyond her Brodie counterpart. If she could have met Miss Brodie, Miss Kay would have put the fictional character firmly in her place.

Even without this, however, we would not have been able to transfer the author's assessment of the real person to the fictional one. For one thing, even an author cannot be regarded as an utterly reliable guide to his or her own book: what an author says about it is always interesting and to be taken into account, but not to be regarded as the last word. Muriel Spark and this novel, as it happens, accidentally provided a particularly clear instance of this general truth. In the course of writing a critical essay on the novel, Isobel Murray of Aberdeen University discovered facts that appear to have contributed to Spark's choice of the name 'Marcia

Blaine' for her fictional school, which we know to have been based on Spark's own school, James Gillespie's. It appears that there was a nineteenth-century American journalist and statesman by the name of James Gillespie Blain, a fact which the author must have come across and used jokingly to devise a new name for her old school. In the course of a subsequent discussion between Murray and Spark, in which this 'discovery' was put to the author for final confirmation, Muriel Spark refused to do so.

It isn't that an author is being awkward or deliberately misleading on such a point: authors' memories are fallible like everyone else's, and they can be either forgetful or mistaken when they look back over decades. That is true both of details of fact (like the James Gillespie Blain matter) and of details of interpretation. In the essay in *The New Yorker*, Spark confesses to a very similar doubt about an even more surprising detail, the choice of the name of the central character: 'I do not know exactly why I chose the name Miss Brodie. But recently I learned that Charlotte Rule, a young American woman who taught me to read when I was three, had been a Miss Brodie and a schoolteacher before her marriage. Could I have heard this fact and recorded it unconsciously?'

Even without such illustrations, however, of Muriel Spark's fallibility as a guide to her book and its origins, we should have to give up any hope of turning to the author for final help in interpretion. Despite its resemblances to actuality, fiction is always its own world, self-contained and finally making sense (if at all) without reference outside itself. As Muriel Spark herself says, elsewhere, fiction is a lie from which, at best, a truth emerges. Each time a book is read afresh, a new (and inevitably failing) attempt to reach that truth is being made. Jean Brodie is likely to be forever just outside our reach. That is one reason why the book stands up so well to reading and rereading.

SANDY STRANGER AND THE BRODIE SET

Two Heroines? – Jean Brodie and Sandy

Everyone retains a vivid impression of Jean Brodie, whether they
have read the book or have seen a dramatisation of it: that
magnetic and contradictory personality grips our imaginations,
just as it does those of the schoolgirls. Nevertheless, when one
rereads the book and starts to think about it, it becomes clear that
Sandy Stranger is just as central and important a character as
Jean Brodie herself. This is not just because whoever betrays
Jean Brodie is bound to be prominent. Rather, the story focuses on
her just as much as it does on the teacher; they share Muriel
Spark's concern equally.

The story is of their interrelationship or, rather, of Sandy's
developing perception of Miss Brodie. We can feel how both are
central to the book's pattern at various points, but perhaps
especially at the beginning and the end. The opening section, up
to 'the age of chivalry is past' (10), is a beautifully controlled
passage, gently providing the reader with what appears to be a
near random selection of details and anecdotes, but firmly centred
on the girls, stressing both their individuality and their group
identity. As the section progresses, however, Miss Brodie becomes
more and more prominent within it, steadily coming to dominate
the reader's attention.

First, it is just her surname, and it is used with reference not
to her but to the group of girls: 'These girls formed the Brodie set'.
Then she becomes 'Miss Brodie', but still she is being reflected
through the unexpected knowledge which she has imparted to the
girls, rather than through direct contact with the reader. A couple
of paragraphs of this, however, serve to give us a very vivid, if
intrigued, sense of her, and by the end of the fourth paragraph she
is 'Jean Brodie', as if to confirm her independent status as a
character in her own right. This point having been reached, the
narrator can break off to tell us a little about the school and its
history before turning to the girls as individuals. It is not long,
however, before Miss Brodie re-enters, as if the girls cannot be
talked about without reference to her. And just as they are being
talked about as individuals, so we are suddenly given Miss
Brodie's own voice in a scrap of classroom conversation (7). The
girls cannot be discussed without Jean Brodie taking over the
discussion. Even before she enters the book in her own right, Jean

Brodie's role and personality is being created for us by the whole movement of the unfolding narration.

Despite this, it looks as if the girls are going to be allowed their own independent life after all, as we begin to listen to the youthful, shy sexual sparring between them and the boys. The association is fragile, however, and breaks apart at the approach of 'a teacher' – Miss Brodie, of course, who wastes no time in dismissing both the boys and Joyce Emily Hammond, in whom she has no interest. (It is only in retrospect that we realise how fateful this moment is: this is the very first contact between Jean Brodie and Joyce Emily Hammond. The girl will be influenced by this teacher to go off to Spain where she will meet her death; the teacher's 'betrayal' will be triggered off by her future involvement with this girl who is so easily dismissed. The author's beautiful control over the book's structure is firm and decisive, even though it is well concealed within the relaxed, seemingly casual mood of the opening. It is not at all obvious that something decisive is beginning here, but, as it turns out, it is. If at one important level the tale that is told is that of the relationship between Jean Brodie and Sandy Stranger, at another, more superficial level, the tale that is told depends on the relationship between Jean Brodie and Joyce Emily Hammond.)

Now that both the girls and Miss Brodie are before us in the current 'now' of the book, we can observe their interaction directly. It is the teacher, of course, who dominates the conversation, not just taking the lead as teachers usually do in informal, out-of-hours conversations with pupils, but imposing her demands and personality on them to an extraordinary extent. The conversation centres on the (to us) new and interesting information about plots against Miss Brodie and has its own structure as the individuality of the girls shrivels and the teacher dominates more and more. As the boys move away, the girls are still being mentioned as individuals: 'Sandy looked with her little screwed-up eyes at Monica's very red nose ...', and Jenny makes her ineffectual little bid for independent action. After a few sentences, however, of Miss Brodie's self-obsessed monologue, the girls become 'the Brodie set' once again. In the context of this fascinating glimpse of dire plottings in the staff room and hints of the heroic in Jean Brodie's 'dark Roman profile', the reference to Rose and her being 'famous for sex-appeal' fails to retrieve for her anything much in the way of individuality – Rose's 'fame' just becomes (once again) her membership ticket for the Brodie set. By the end of the passage, the girls have just become 'everyone' and are playing second-fiddle to Jean Brodie's ringing statements about her prime and about the age of chivalry being past. Once again, Muriel Spark has so written this seemingly casual bit of dialogue as to enact, through it, the nature of the teacher and her relationship with her girls. The opening section of the book is strung out between the two, and is written so as to convey a deep sense of the teacher insinuating herself into a position of dominance in their lives.

If the opening is designed in one way to suggest that the relationship between teacher and pupils is the essential subject-matter of the book, the ending manages to sum that up even more effectively and concisely. After Sandy has suddenly found out about Miss Brodie's influence on Joyce Emily Hammond and the decision to go to Spain, the narrative moves instantly to the scene of betrayal. This is in turn handled with maximum conciseness (as if to play down its natural tendency to be the climax of the novel – once again, Muriel Spark wants to retain the strength of the usual narrative patterns while making them far less obvious than usual) and moves on immediately to the departure of Sandy from Edinburgh – information which inevitably serves to suggest the end of a major phase in her life, and in the story itself. Everything else in the last few pages is apparently just a tail-piece, beginning with the information about Jean Brodie's enforced retiral.

In these last paragraphs, Miss Brodie seems to fade away in a movement which reverses the process of her entry into the book. She is given three whole paragraphs of direct speech (125–126), as if to suggest that she is still important as an individual – but it is only an illusion of direct speech, for this is a letter to Sandy and the 'conversation' between them here is on paper, not face to face. Jean Brodie is beginning to recede, to exist only on paper, in other people's reports of her, and in Sandy's memory. The bulk of her letter seems to be a survey of the 'set', but by now we have such a strong sense of these girls as individuals that they no longer seem such a simple group and consequently Miss Brodie, the focus of the group, can be seen more and more to be living in the past. Her ideas about these girls no longer match up with reality, as can be seen by comparing her suspicions about them (to say nothing of her mistaken sense of security as regards Sandy) with the varying degrees of respect and regard that Jenny, Eunice and Monica show in the following page. These three, with their different memories and information, convey a sense of Miss Brodie as something past and gone, though permanently present in their

memories and affections. Yet through these snatches of conversation, Sandy is emerging to occupy the final position of
dominance: she stands apart from the other three in her certain
knowledge of the betrayer's identity and in the unspoken intensity
of her sense of her own relationship with the dead woman whose
life she had wrecked. The scene is set for the final movement (the
conversation with the 'inquiring young man') towards that won-
derfully judged final line, 'Sandy said: "There was a Miss Jean
Brodie in her prime."' At first glance, Jean Brodie is made the
final focus. At second glance, the focus is on Sandy's awareness of
the centrality of Jean Brodie in her own life. The two come
together as one in a line which is as memorably powerful as it is
plain and clear: Sandy's sense of Jean Brodie is the single,
unifying subject of the book.

The World of the Brodie Set

The pleasure in encountering Jean Brodie is not the only reason
why the book is so immediately entertaining for readers, although
it is perhaps the principal one. Almost as important in creating
the fun of the book, however, is the picture that it gives of the
inner lives and thoughts of young, adolescent girls. Much of the
interest of this part of the book depends, of course, on our more
experienced and worldly-wise sense of how inexperienced and (at
times) comically mistaken the young schoolgirls can be: their
speculations, in the second chapter, about the practicalities of sex
are the clearest and most obvious example of this. In a different
mood is Sandy's fear of some of the things she encounters during
the walk through the Old Town of Edinburgh: she has a shrinking,
innocent reaction to things to which most of the readers are
hardened. Most modern readers, in their more certain knowledge
of the ways of the world, inevitably feel superior to these very
young and very sheltered people trying to make sense of adult
things for the first time.

Yet if we partly feel superior, do we not also feel that there is a
great and refreshing truthfulness about Muriel Spark's depiction
of the girls' thoughts and emotions? One of the things which helps
organise and shape our feelings about the book is that it is rather
different from other, older and more traditional books about
school life. There is a very familiar form of 'school story', usually
involving a group of schoolboys or girls at a private boarding
school. Such stories tend to be concerned with various unlikely

'adventures' concerning villainous fellow-pupils, or unpopular teachers, or local petty criminals, or (if the story has a wartime setting) incompetent German spies. In other words, such stories are essentially very artificial, being set in a play-world where few of the problems and feelings of real life intrude. When they are set in boarding schools, as they usually are, such tales seem to take place in a cut-off, cloistered world with its own rules and concerns sharing little with the everyday lives of ordinary people. In particular, such traditional school stories would never contain such things as, 'In later years, sex was only one of the things in life. That year it was everything' (44), let alone have a schoolgirl say, on the topic of finding out about sex, 'I feel I'm past it' (80)! A large part of the freshness of Muriel Spark's book comes from our instinctive realisation that this novel is a very unorthodox, unconventional treatment of subject-matter about which very strong fictional conventions had been established.

The world of Marcia Blaine School for Girls is generally very different from the stereotype fictional girls' school and the general preoccupations of the girls are not those depicted in the usual schoolgirl stories. In part, of course, this is due to the unorthodox behaviour of one prominent teacher. We can well believe that teachers like Miss Mackay and Miss Lockhart would fit perfectly well in the usual story-book school: that would be entirely in tune with their tendency towards the safe and conventional. (Indeed, Marcia Blaine School, with all its paraphernalia of houses and its attempts to instil a sense of team-spirit, is trying to be a school of exactly that sort.) Miss Brodie, on the other hand, has certainly given her girls some very unusual pieces of information (the Buchmanites, the interior decoration of A.A. Milne's London house, et cetera).

We do not feel, however, that their knowingness and curiosity about life has all been due to her. Indeed, in many passages in which Miss Brodie's classroom teaching is depicted, we feel that the girls, as well as the reader, are watching a rather strange one-woman show which only really convinces Miss Brodie herself. The girls simply adapt to her classroom ways and learn the right responses:

> '... discretion is...discretion is...Sandy?'
> 'The better part of valour, Miss Brodie.' (47)

Her undoubted influence over them does not really depend on the information she gives them in class; it arises from the person that

she is. Even then, however, we do not feel that her influence is the
sole (or even the main) determining factor which dictates how the
girls will turn out. For the real departure from the usual school
story convention concerns not so much Jean Brodie (rather weird
teachers can occasionally appear in even the most orthodox school
story) but in the treatment of the thoughts and concerns of the
girls themselves – thoughts and concerns which essentially arise
from their own adolescent natures rather than being put there by
any teacher.

The Strangeness of Sandy Stranger

If this is true of the Brodie set as a whole, it is especially true of
Sandy. While the set has no clear leader (and that in itself is one
difference between this novel and the typical school novel) Sandy
is always securely at its centre, especially as Miss Brodie grad-
ually homes in on her as her especial favourite. She is the nearest
the set gets to having a leader, but she is very different indeed
from her counterparts in standard school stories: in those, the
group leader is distinguished by qualities of personality which
make him or her a cross between a managing director and a
platoon commander. Sandy has no such obvious personal traits:
she is 'famous' only for her vowel sounds, but 'notorious' for 'her
small, almost non-existent, eyes' (7). These are among the few
prominent things which outwardly distinguish her; another is her
slightly strange name. One wonders why Muriel Spark has given
her these rather peculiar characteristics?

As always in this novel, there is no simple and obvious answer
to this, or to any other questions which it prompts. We might say
the following, however. Her surname suggests, perhaps, both
someone who is 'strange' (eccentric) and who is 'estranged' (dis-
tanced, alienated). It is not that her behaviour or personality is
strongly like either of these things for the bulk of the book – while
at school she is sociable and normal with everyone she associates
with – yet the hints within her surname point, we might think, to
the unexpectedly strong and individual actions of her later years:
betraying Miss Brodie and entering a secluded convent. Both
involve a rejection. In betraying Jean Brodie she is rejecting not
only someone who had been very friendly to her, but also her own
schoolgirl past, and (to some extent) the group allegiances of her
schooldays. In entering the convent she is rejecting the world. She
has estranged herself from much of her past life. She has also

turned out to be 'stranger' (that is, more mysterious, more capable of astonishing surprises) than any of the other characters thought. She is the opposite of obvious, easily knowable, safely familiar.

'Sandy' is harder still. The main reason for its choice, I suspect, is that it is less predictably and unarguably a girl's name than those of any of the others (Monica, Rose, Jenny, Eunice, Mary). In retrospect, it seems to confirm that potential for separateness which both the surname, and Sandy's actions later in the book, imply more directly. It seems suitable for a girl who proves less easy to pigeon-hole than any of the others: the sexual ambiguity of the name makes us feel, perhaps, just a little less at ease with her. Beyond that, one might be tempted to think that 'Sandy' suggests a certain dryness, a certain aridity of temperament, which might fit with her detached ruthlessness in betraying Jean Brodie – and also with the rather bleak and maybe unsatisfying life which she eventually chooses for herself. These are mere possibilities, however.

The small eyes which are her main claim to notoriety (the long vowels which are also mentioned at the outset are less prominent in our sense of her) draw attention to her powerful tendency towards observation of others – and also hint, we might say, at the piercing, analytical intelligence which she brings to bear in her observations. (Small, deep-set eyes suggest a narrow, piercing, discriminating gaze, whereas large, prominent eyes would have hinted at a wide, all-embracing, rather thoughtless stare.) There may also be a paradoxical suggestion of near-blindness, certainly of great narrowness, in the image of her tiny eyes. If so, this may be a hinted judgement by the author on her and on what she does. A detail such as this of Sandy's eyes carries the strong suggestion of being a signal from the author to the reader. They are, in a sense, extraneous to the story – the smallness of her eyes does not play a part *within* the tale by, say, warping her personality because she is self-conscious of her appearance. It is a detail which comes in the same category as the western movie convention of white hats for good guys and black hats for villains: it expresses information about a character by a means other than showing the character in action. Where the convention of the hats is crudely obvious, however, the implications both of Sandy's name and of her strange eyes are a good deal more subtle.

Sandy, however. These stories and daydreams are, for the girls,
indirect (and therefore safe) ways of confronting the possibilities
they are glimpsing about adult life in general and about the lives
of their parents and teachers in particular. Occasionally, it is true,
they try directly to imagine these grown-ups doing adult things.
Such attempts are often funny, but they are often failures as well,
as when Sandy and Jenny attempt to visualise the process by
which Teddy Lloyd got his wife pregnant (17). They concentrate
on the art master's marriage rather than on the sexual activities
of their own parents, which understandably they find too difficult
to cope with at all, but even with the Lloyds they dissolve in
giggles and have to retreat to more abstract speculations. In a
way, the whole story of the novel is of Sandy's struggle to reconcile
her intellectual realisation that Jean Brodie has a sex-life with
the impossibility of realising it imaginatively. 'It was impossible to
imagine Miss Brodie sleeping with Mr Lowther, it was impossible
to imagine her in a sexual context at all, and yet it was impossible
not to suspect that such things were so.' (61) Sandy, more
imaginative and intelligent than the rest of the girls, has been put
in an impossible position by Jean Brodie's bringing of her own
emotional life into the classroom. This is the dilemma which
brings about the whole shape of Sandy's life.

Spinning Yarns and Telling Tales

The girls are driven to keep trying to understand the adult reality
of the grown-ups with whom they are in contact (especially their
teacher), and so Sandy and Jenny embark on their work of fiction
based on the image of Miss Brodie's lost love (18–19). What is
striking about this, of course, is how little contact it retains with
any of the actual reality of its characters: it is simply a fragment
of girlish romantic fantasy – an adventure story with suggestions
of R.L. Stevenson, Lord Byron, and some of the more colourful
episodes from Scottish history (like Catherine Douglas's valiant
attempt to save James I from assassination by barring a door with
her own arm). Muriel Spark catches the style of such stuff
superbly: 'I swear to you before all I hold sacred ...', 'Well do I
know that yon girl Jenny ...', 'Her large eyes flashed with an
azure light of appeal.'
    In another sense, it is Sandy who catches the style so well: she
is much better than Jenny at writing it. Indeed, we soon realise
that Sandy has a particularly active and vivid fantasy life, and

that Muriel Spark is singling out this feature of Sandy as a person as one of the key elements in her nature. Nor is her ability to imagine these mental episodes to be distinguished from her skill in catching the appropriate verbal style for each of them. A major part of Sandy's skill is her ability to find the right words for her daydream characters. As she grows up, Sandy becomes a gifted inventor of tales, and a skilled manipulator of verbal styles.

Yet she has had a good teacher, of course. It is one of the similarities between Sandy and Jean Brodie that they both have such pronounced tendencies to imaginatively intermingle real life and imaginative life. It is one of the things which Sandy notices about Miss Brodie, as she discusses yet again her slain beloved:

> This was the first time the girls had heard of Hugh's artistic leanings. Sandy puzzled over this and took counsel with Jenny, and it came to them both that Miss Brodie was making her new love story fit the old. ... Sandy was fascinated by this method of making patterns with facts... (72)

Each of the two leading characters is a tale-teller, or (to put it another way) an author of fiction. And fiction is imagined, in this novel, as consisting of making patterns with facts – which is what Spark herself is doing with a vengeance as she writes. She seems to be perceiving a contrast between real-life content and abstract pattern. This is the contrast which is given particular prominence in the scene of the girls' art lesson with Teddy Lloyd during which they dissolve in giggles when confronted with Botticelli's *Primavera* (49–50). The schoolgirls react to what they see as dancing women in transparent drapery which shows their bottoms; Lloyd and Jean Brodie treat the whole thing as an abstract pattern of lines and design. The teachers continue their denial of the human content of art when they proceed to look at a Madonna and Child, which Lloyd discusses in terms of 'what the painter had done with his brush' with a detachment which shocks the children who had instinctively expected at least some acknowledgement of the sacred nature of the subject. In this scene, the giggling girls are perhaps not simply the annoyingly immature creatures their teachers seem to think they are: their reactions are very human and contrast with the almost unnatural coldness of the teachers' way of approaching art. Spark is admitting, as it were, that art contains (and needs) pattern and technique but seems to be implying, too, that human feelings about what art

SCOTNOTES

Study guides to major Scottish writers and literary texts

Produced by the Schools and Further Education Committee
of the Association for Scottish Literary Studies

Series Editors
Lorna Borrowman Smith
Ronald Renton

THE ASSOCIATION FOR SCOTTISH LITERARY STUDIES aims to promote the study, teaching and writing of Scottish literature, and to further the study of the languages of Scotland.

To these ends, the ASLS publishes works of Scottish literature; literary criticism and in-depth reviews of Scottish books in *Scottish Studies Review*; short articles, features and news in *ScotLit*; and scholarly studies of language in *Scottish Language*. It also publishes *New Writing Scotland*, an annual anthology of new poetry, drama and short fiction, in Scots, English and Gaelic. ASLS has also prepared a range of teaching materials covering Scottish language and literature for use in schools.

All the above publications are available in return for an annual subscription. Schools can receive teaching materials by joining ASLS at a special reduced rate. Enquiries should be sent to:

ASLS, c/o Department of Scottish History, 9 University Gardens, University of Glasgow, Glasgow G12 8QH.

Telephone/fax +44 (0)141 330 5309
e mail d.jones@asls.org.uk
www.asls.org.uk